FIERCE | The Biblical Account of How David Slew Goliath

© 2016 Adalis Shuttlesworth

ISBN - 978-0-9981753-0-0

Revival Today
PO Box 254
Oakdale, PA, 15071
RevivalToday.com

Illustrated by Justin Stewart
Justifii.com

For information about special discounts available for bulk purchases, sales promotions, fund-raising and educational needs, contact Revival Today Sales at 412-787-2578 or info@revivaltoday.com

DISCLAIMER:
This is **NOT** the Bible. Read your Bible!

FIERCE

The Biblical Account Of How David Slew Goliath

by

ADALIS SHUTTLESWORTH

illustrated by

JUSTIN STEWART

REVIVAL TODAY

TO THE MIGHTY:

_____

FROM:

_____

DATE:

_____

A LETTER TO PARENTS

I am beyond excited to share this series with you! As a mother, I fully understand the need for a more precise understanding of biblical principles. Our children do not need a watered down version of The Bible. They are brilliant, unaffected by doubt, and not jaded. Now is the time to begin to instill principles that will impact them for the rest of their lives. They can learn now that they don't have to live in fear. They don't have to deal with the issues of this world; they can rise above them and be victorious like David!

ABOUT THE MIGHTY SERIES

The Mighty Series is a compilation of children's books taken directly from the Word of God without the side of political correctness. There isn't a junior Holy Spirit for kids; they can walk in the fullness of their calling and destiny right now. The Bible says in Joel 2:28, "Your sons and daughters will prophecy..." The Bible is filled with promises for our children! As you read these books to them, know that you are ministering to their spirits, and building them up to be everything God has called them to be!

THE STORY OF DAVID AND
GOLIATH CAN BE FOUND IN

1 SAMUEL 17

**T**he Israelites stood at the edge of their camp in terror. A nine-foot tall giant named Goliath came out of the enemy's camp.

"CHOOSE ONE MAN TO FIGHT ME! IF HE WINS, WE WILL BE YOUR SLAVES, BUT, IF I WIN, YOU WILL BE OUR SLAVES!"

he said. No Israelite dared come against the giant named Goliath.

For **40 DAYS** and **40 NIGHTS** Goliath came out of his tent so all could see him.

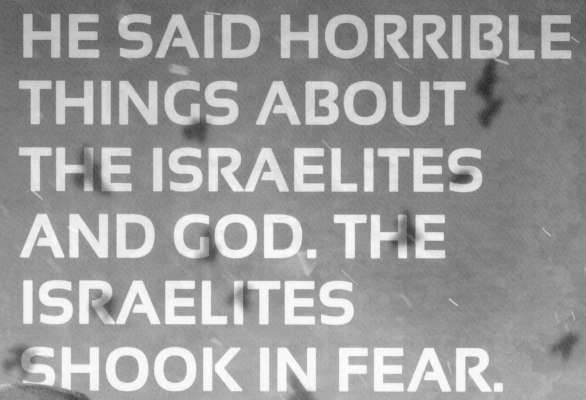

HE SAID HORRIBLE THINGS ABOUT THE ISRAELITES AND GOD. THE ISRAELITES SHOOK IN FEAR.

Back in Bethlehem, little David was helping take care of his father Jesse's sheep.

DAVID LOVED GOD WITH ALL HIS HEART.

Many times, David would sing songs and worship God in the fields with the sheep. He was completely devoted to God.

"DAVID, TAKE THIS BASKET OF BREAD AND CHEESE TO YOUR BROTHERS. IT'S BEEN SO LONG, GO SEE HOW THEY'RE DOING,"

Jesse said. David left the sheep behind and took off to check on his brothers.

By the time David got to the battlefield, the armies were facing each other.

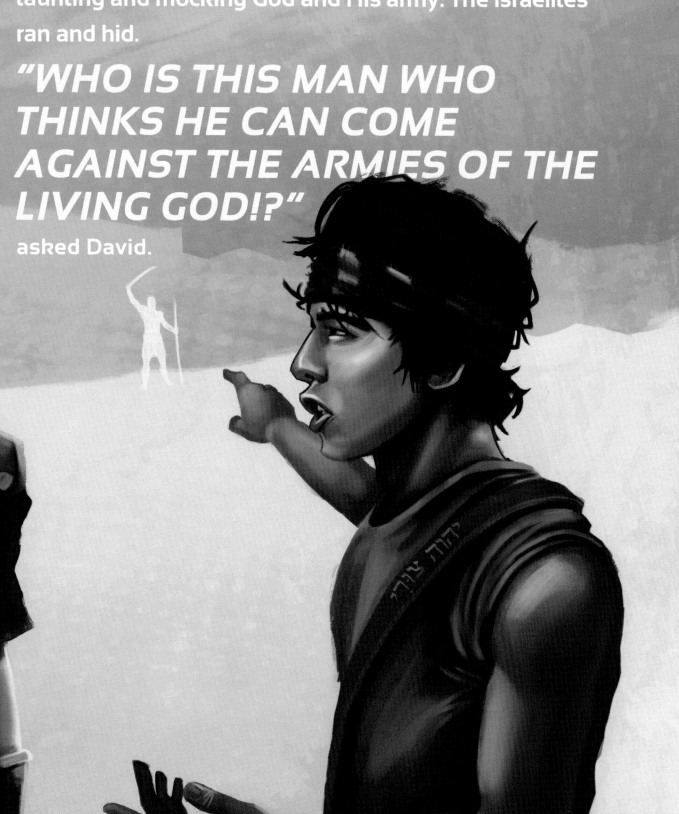

As usual, Goliath made his way to the battlefront, taunting and mocking God and His army. The Israelites ran and hid.

"WHO IS THIS MAN WHO THINKS HE CAN COME AGAINST THE ARMIES OF THE LIVING GOD!?"

asked David.

Saul, King of Israel, overheard David's boldness. "I'll fight him and take him out!" David declared. "Are you crazy!? You're just a boy, David. Goliath is an expert soldier. You won't be able to stand against him!" King Saul exclaimed.

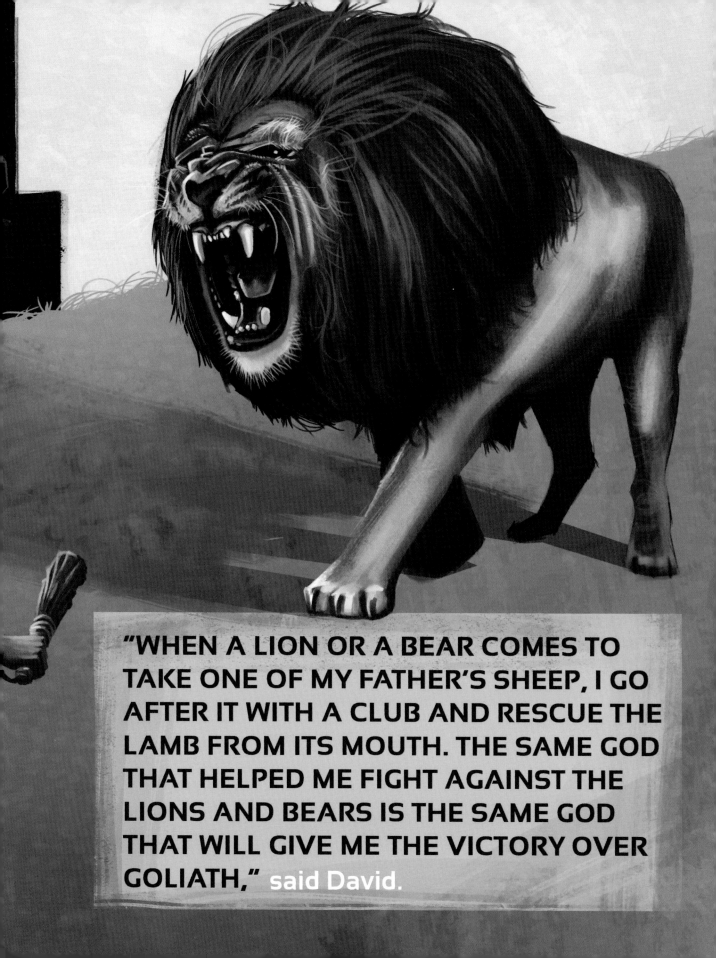

"WHEN A LION OR A BEAR COMES TO TAKE ONE OF MY FATHER'S SHEEP, I GO AFTER IT WITH A CLUB AND RESCUE THE LAMB FROM ITS MOUTH. THE SAME GOD THAT HELPED ME FIGHT AGAINST THE LIONS AND BEARS IS THE SAME GOD THAT WILL GIVE ME THE VICTORY OVER GOLIATH," said David.

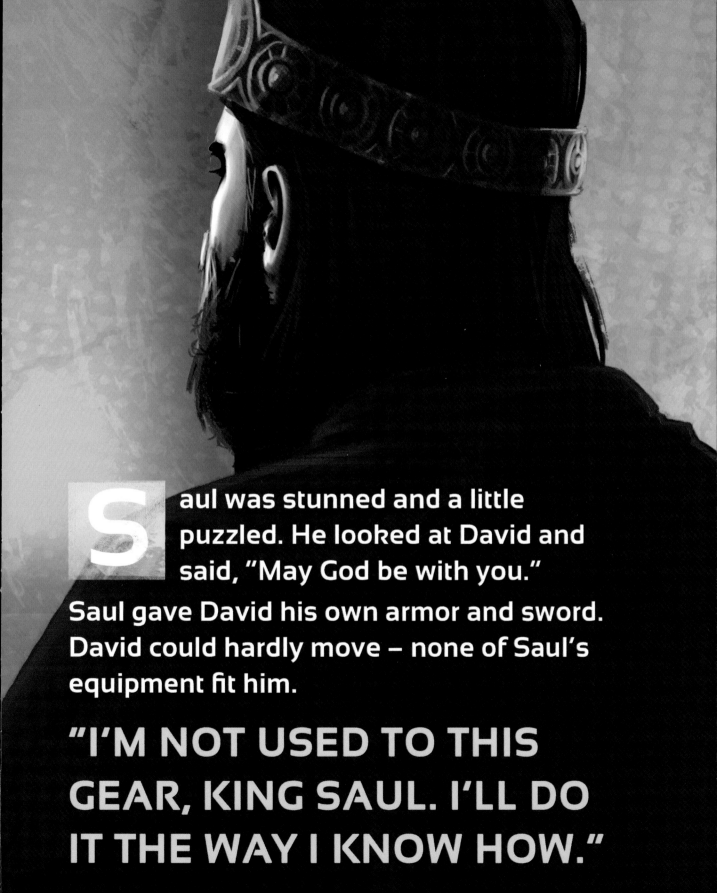

Saul was stunned and a little puzzled. He looked at David and said, "May God be with you."

Saul gave David his own armor and sword. David could hardly move – none of Saul's equipment fit him.

"I'M NOT USED TO THIS GEAR, KING SAUL. I'LL DO IT THE WAY I KNOW HOW."

**D**avid dropped Saul's armor and began to search for five smooth stones by the stream.

HE PUT THE STONES INTO HIS SHEPHERD'S BAG AND, WITH ONLY A STAFF AND A SLING, DAVID BEGAN TO LOOK FOR GOLIATH.

**G**oliath walked toward David and said, "Am I a dog, that you come at me with sticks?"

David replied,

"YOU COME TO ME WITH A SWORD, BUT I COME TO YOU IN THE NAME OF THE LORD!

Today, the Lord will conquer you, and everyone here will see what happens when you come against the God of Israel."

David continued, "Today, the Lord will conquer you, and I will kill you and cut off your head. Then, all will know that God rescues His people!"

As Goliath walked closer to attack David, David ran quickly to meet him. David reached into his shepherd's bag and pulled out one smooth stone.

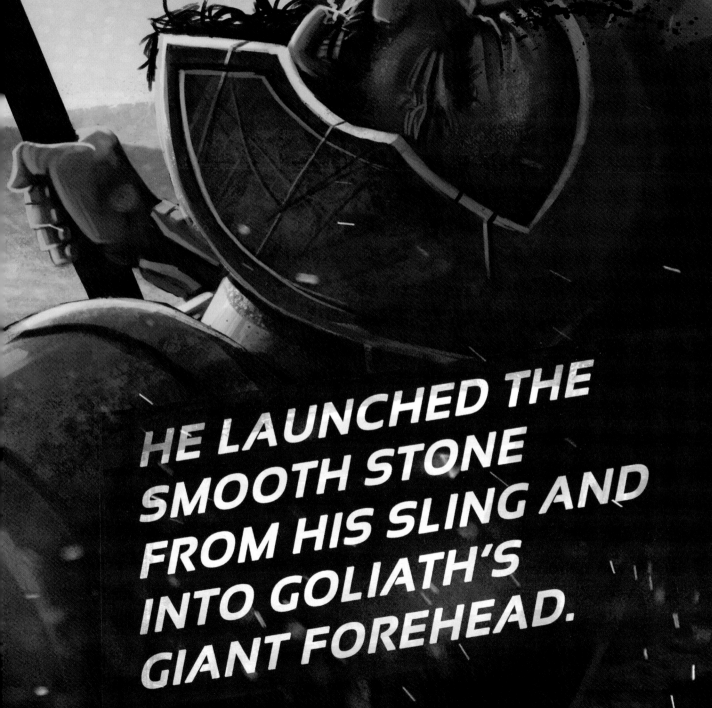

HE LAUNCHED THE SMOOTH STONE FROM HIS SLING AND INTO GOLIATH'S GIANT FOREHEAD.

GOLIATH THUDDED FACEDOWN ON THE GROUND.

David ran to the giant body and used Goliath's sword to kill him. The Philistines saw this and ran away in terror.

That day, God gave little David the giant victory over his enemy Goliath.

ABC's of Salvation

Have you ever asked Jesus into your heart? Jesus said in John 14:6- "I am the way. And I am the truth and the life. The only way to the Father is through me". If you want to live a life of love, joy and peace, you need Jesus! How do you accept Jesus into your heart? It's as easy as A-B-C!

ADMIT that you need Jesus in your life. The Bible says in Romans 3:23, "All people have sinned and are not good enough for God's glory." Sin is the thing that blocks God from our lives. That's why God sent His Son, Jesus-- to forgive us of all the bad things we've done.

BELIEVE that Jesus is God's son, sent to this earth to die on the cross for your sins, your healing and your success.

CONFESS Jesus as your savior! The Bible says in Romans 10:9, that "If you declare with your mouth, "Jesus is Lord," and if you believe in your heart that God raised Jesus from death, then you will be saved."

It's So Simple!
Pray This after me.

Heavenly Father,

Forgive me of all my sins. Come into my heart wash me clean. Today, I make you my Savior, Lord and Friend. I am forgiven. I am a child of God. I am Mighty through Jesus Christ.

In Jesus' Name. Amen!

If you've prayed this prayer and accepted Jesus as your Lord, Savior and friend email us at:

info@themightyseries.com

and we will send you bible and a gift.

HooraaaY!!

ADALIS SHUTTLESWORTH
FOUNDER & AUTHOR OF THE MIGHTY SERIES